Vinegar

Tips for household

A collection of fantastic uses for vinegar around the home!

(im)PulsePaperbacks

Vinegar is one of nature's most diverse products - although many of us only associate it only with cooking or putting on chips! It has a fascinating history dating back centuries, when the Ancients very quickly uncovered the tremendous versatility of vinegar with some reports suggesting that it was used as a cleaning and preserving agent as long ago as in Babylonian times. It is also reported that Caesar's armies used vinegar as a beverage, that the Egyptian queen Cleopatra used it to win a bet and that the often suggested greatest beauty of all time, Helen of Troy, bathed in vinegar to relax!

Vinegar came to the rescue in the Middle Ages in some extraordinary ways. During the Black Plague in Europe, thieves poured vinegar over their skin to protect themselves from germs before robbing the dead! During the seventeenth century in Europe and England vinegar was used as a deodorizer when women conveniently carried vinegar-laden sponges in small silver boxes and men stored them in their walking canes! It is also reported that people would hold vinegar to their noses to reduce the smell of raw sewage in the streets. Even the British Navy used vinegar to preserve food during long sea voyages and to clean the decks of their ships.

In modern times vinegar continues to play a valuable role in society. During the first world war, vinegar was used to treat wounds on the battlefields and nowadays, white vinegar is recommended for the treatment of rashes, bites and other minor ailments - particularly useful if you are camping as it has a multitude of uses.

Vinegar has become most popular, however, as a condiment on chips and as an ingredient in food and baking. The virtues of speciality vinegars, such as balsamic and rice vinegars are proclaimed with increasing passion by food connoisseurs and vinegar is still, of course, used for commercial and domestic pickling and preserving.

For centuries women have used white vinegar for cleaning and have passed down their usage tips through their family. However, in our time-pressed world many of the great and varied uses for vinegar have been forgotten. This book provides a broad range of vinegar usage tips that are convenient to use and that really work.

Vinegar as a cost effective and environmentally friendly cleaning agent is becoming increasingly popular. The advantages to the purse, the planet and our health, compared to toxic cleaners, speak for themselves.

> "Men are like wine — some turn to vinegar, but the best improve with age."
>
> Pope John XXIII (1881-1963)

Types of Vinegar

White

So-called "white vinegar" (actually transparent in appearance) can be made by oxidizing a distilled alcohol. Alternatively, it may be nothing more than a solution of acetic acid in water. Most commercial white vinegars are 5 acetic acid solutions. They are made from grain (often maize) and water. White vinegar is used for culinary as well as cleaning purposes.

Malt

Malt vinegar is made by malting barley, causing the starch in the grain to turn to maltose. An ale is then brewed from the maltose and allowed to turn into vinegar, which is then aged. It is typically light brown in colour. A cheaper alternative, called "non-brewed condiment," is a solution of 4-8% acetic acid coloured with caramel. There is also around 1-3% citric acid present. Non-brewed condiment is more popular in the North of England, and gained popularity with the rise of the Temperance Societies. The non-alcoholic nature of non-brewed condiment therefore makes it popular for individuals whose cultural or religious beliefs forbid them from drinking alcohol.

Wine

Wine vinegar is made from red or white wine, and is the most commonly used vinegar in Mediterranean countries and Germany. As with wine, there is a considerable range in quality. Better quality wine vinegars are matured in wood for up to two years and exhibit a complex, mellow flavour. There are more expensive wine vinegars made from individual varieties of wine, such as champagne, sherry, or pinot grigio.

Apple cider

Apple cider vinegar, sometimes known simply as cider vinegar, is made from cider or apple must, and is often sold unfiltered, with a brownish-yellow colour. It is currently very popular, partly due to its beneficial health and beauty properties.

Fruit

Fruit vinegars are made from fruit wines without any additional flavouring. Common flavours of fruit vinegar include blackcurrant, raspberry, quince and tomato. Typically, the flavours of the original fruits remain tasteable in the final vinegar.

Most such vinegars are produced in Europe, where there is a growing market for high priced vinegars made solely from specific fruits (as opposed to non-fruit vinegars which are infused with fruits or fruit flavours). Persimmon vinegar is popular in South Korea, and jujube vinegar is produced in China. Umeboshi vinegar, a salty, sour liquid that is a by-product of umeboshi (pickled ume) production, is produced in Japan but is technically not a true vinegar.

Balsamic

Balsamic vinegar is an aromatic, aged type of vinegar traditionally manufactured in Modena, Italy, from the concentrated juice, or must, of white grapes (typically of the Trebbiano variety). It is very dark brown in colour and its flavour is rich, sweet, and complex, with the finest grades being the end product of years of aging in a successive number of casks made of various types of wood (including oak, mulberry, chestnut, cherry, juniper, ash, and acacia). Originally an artisanal product available only to the Italian upper classes, balsamic vinegar became widely known and available around the world in the late 20th century. True balsamic is aged between 3 and 12 years and is expensive. The commercial balsamic sold in supermarkets is typically made with red wine vinegar or concentrated grape juice mixed with a strong vinegar which is laced with caramel and sugar. However produced, balsamic needs to be made from a grape product. Balsamic has a high acid level, but the sweetness covers the tart flavour, making it very mellow.

Rice

Rice vinegar is most popular in the cuisines of East and Southeast Asia. It is available in white (actually light yellow), red, and black variants. The Japanese prefer a light and more delicate rice vinegar for the preparation of sushi rice. Red rice vinegar is traditionally coloured with red yeast rice, although some Chinese brands use artificial food colouring instead. Black rice vinegar is most popular in China, although it is also produced in Japan (see East Asian black). It may be used as a substitute for balsamic vinegar, although its dark colour and the fact that it is aged may be the only similarity between the two products. Some varieties of rice vinegar are sweetened or otherwise seasoned with spices or other added flavourings.

Coconut

Coconut vinegar, made from the sap, or "toddy," of the coconut palm, is used extensively in Southeast Asian cuisine (particularly in the Philippines, a major producer of the product), as well as in some cuisines of India. A cloudy white liquid, it has a particularly sharp, acidic taste with a slightly yeasty note.

Cane

Cane vinegar, made from sugar cane juice, is most popular in the Ilocos Region of the northern Philippines (where it is called sukang iloko), although it is also produced in France and the United States. It ranges from dark yellow to golden brown in colour and has a mellow flavour, similar in some respects to rice vinegar, though with a somewhat "fresher" taste. Contrary to expectation, it is not sweeter than other vinegars, containing no residual sugar.

Raisin

Vinegar made from raisins is used in cuisines of the Middle East, and is produced in Turkey. It is cloudy and medium brown in colour, with a mild flavour.

Date

Vinegar made from dates is a traditional product of the Middle East.

Beer

Vinegar made from beer is produced in Germany, Austria, and the Netherlands. Although its flavour depends on the particular type of beer from which it is made, it is often described as having a malty taste. That produced in Bavaria is a light golden colour, with a very sharp and not overly complex flavour.

Honey

Vinegar made from honey is rare, though commercially available honey vinegars are produced in Italy and France.

East Asian black

Chinese black vinegar is an aged product made from rice, wheat, millet, or sorghum, or a combination thereof. It has an inky black colour and a complex, malty flavour. There is no fixed recipe and thus some Chinese black vinegars may contain added sugar, spices, or caramel colour. The most popular variety, Chinkiang vinegar, originated in the city of Zhenjiang, in the eastern coastal province of Jiangsu, China, and is also produced in Tianjin and Hong Kong. A somewhat lighter form of black vinegar, made from rice, is also produced in Japan, where it is called kurozu. Since 2004 it has been marketed as a healthful drink; its manufacturers claim that it contains high concentrations of amino acids.

Flavoured vinegars

Popular fruit-flavoured vinegars include those infused with whole raspberries, blueberries, or figs (or else from flavourings derived from these fruits). Some of the more exotic fruit-flavoured vinegars include blood orange and pear. Herb vinegars are flavoured with herbs, most commonly Mediterranean herbs such as thyme or oregano. Such vinegars can be prepared at home by adding sprigs of fresh or dried herbs to vinegar bought from shops; generally a light-coloured, mild tasting vinegar such as that made from white wine is used for this purpose. Sweetened vinegar is of Cantonese origin and is made from rice wine, sugar and herbs including ginger, cloves and other spices.

Wash day blues!

Vinegar really is an unsung hero where laundry is concerned, so here are a few hints and tips to help eliminate wash day blues. When using vinegar in laundry, use white distilled vinegar but do not use vinegar if you add bleach to your cycle as this can produce harmful vapours.

Clean your washing machine
An easy way to periodically clean out soap scum and disinfect your washing machine washer is to pour in 450ml (2 cups) of white distilled vinegar, then run the machine through a full cycle without any clothes or detergent.

Fabric conditioning
Instead of expensive fabric conditioners, add 275ml (1/2 pint) of white distilled vinegar to your rinse cycle which will keep your linens soft.

Preventative Measures

Anti-bacterial rinse
If you add 275ml (1/2 pint) of white distilled vinegar to your rinse cycle this will kill any remaining bacteria.

Colour Fading

To brighten your colours, instead of using that costly all-colour bleach, you can get the same results using vinegar. Just add 275ml (1/2 pint) white distilled vinegar to your machine's wash cycle to brighten up the colours in each load.

Colour Running

If you buy a piece of clothing or fabric that you think will run, soak your new garments in a few cups of undiluted white distilled vinegar for 10-15 minutes before their first washing. You can also add 225ml (1 cup) of white distilled vinegar to the last rinse, and that will set the colour of your newly dyed fabrics.

Lint reduction

Add 275ml (1/2 pint) of white distilled vinegar to your rinse cycle and you will notice a dramatic reduction in lint on your clothes.

Make new clothes ready to wear

Get the chemicals, dust, odour, and whatever else out of your brand-new or secondhand clothes by pouring 225ml (1 cup) of white distilled vinegar into the wash cycle the first time you wash them which will increase the life of the garment.

Soap residue

Eliminate soap residue by adding 275ml (1/2 pint) of white distilled vinegar to your rinse cycle.

Static cling

Reduce static cling in clothes by adding 275ml (1/2 pint) of white distilled vinegar to your rinse cycle.

Swimming Costumes

White distilled vinegar is also great for preserving the colour of swimming costumes. Put a little in water and soak your new swimwear, and the colour will last a lot longer even if you swim a lot in pools with lots of chlorine.

Tights

When washing nylon tights, adding white distilled vinegar to the water will prolong their lifespan.

Rescue remedies

Blankets
Wool and cotton blankets come out soft if you add 500ml (approx. 3/4 pint) white distilled vinegar to your rinse cycle.

Get the yellow out of clothing
To restore yellowed clothing, let the garments soak overnight in a solution of 12 parts warm water to 1 part white distilled vinegar. Wash them the following morning.

Shrunken woollens
Shrunken woollen jumpers and other items can usually be stretched back to their original size after washing them in a solution of 1 part white wine vinegar to 2 parts water for 25 minutes. Let the garment air-dry after stretching it.

Whiten Sports Socks
Add 225ml (1 cup) white distilled vinegar to 1.5 litres (approx. 2 1/2 pints) tap water in a large pot. Bring the solution to a boil, then pour it into a bucket and drop in your dingy socks. Let them soak overnight then next day, wash them as you normally would.

Musty odours
When the weather is hot and when a load of laundry doesn't get dried soon enough or fast enough – it gets that musty mildew smell - re-wash the clothes adding 275 ml (1/2 pint) of white distilled vinegar.

Cigarette odour on clothes
To get the lingering smell of cigarette smoke out of your good suit or dress, you can remove the smell without having to take your clothes to the dry cleaner. Just add 275 ml (1/2 pint) of white distilled vinegar to a bathtub filled with the hottest water from your tap. Close the door and hang your garments above the steam. The smell should be gone after a few hours.

Deodorising Wool jumpers
Handwash in luke warm water then rinse in equal parts of white distilled vinegar and water to remove lingering odours.

Diesel Spills
If diesel is spilled on clothes, the smell is horrible and refuses to go away. A little vinegar added to the washer takes most (if not all) the smell out.

Remove bleach odours
If using bleach for stain removal, add 275 ml (1/2 pint) vinegar to the final rinse to remove the bleach smell.

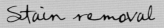

Stain removal

Bloodstains

Treat the stains on your clothing as soon as possible as bloodstains are relatively easy to remove before they dry but can be nearly impossible to wash out after 24 hours. If you can get to the stain before it sets, treat it by pouring full-strength white distilled vinegar on the spot. Let it soak in for 5-10 minutes, then blot well with a cloth or towel. Repeat if necessary, then wash immediately.

Deodorant and perspiration stains

Remove stains from your washable shirts and blouses by gently rubbing the spot with undiluted white distilled vinegar before laundering. Wash in the hottest water that's safe for the fabric.

Dried-in stains

Dried-in stains will often come out in the wash after being pretreated with a solution of 3 tablespoons white distilled vinegar and 2 tablespoons liquid detergent in 1 litre warm water. Rub into the stain, then blot dry before washing.

Grease

If grease is spilt on your clothes and cannot be washed straight away, sprinkle salt over the stain to absorb the grease. When you get home, rub the area with neat detergent and wash as normal. You can also mix one part salt to four parts vinegar and rub on the stain, then wash as normal.

Ink

Treat by first wetting with some white distilled vinegar, then rub in a paste of 2 parts vinegar to 3 parts cornflour. Allow the paste to thoroughly dry before washing the item.

Remove rings from collars and cuffs

Scrub with a paste made from 2 parts white distilled vinegar to 3 parts baking soda. Let the paste set for half an hour before washing.

Sponge out serious stains

Cola, hair dye, ketchup, and wine stains on washable cotton blends should be treated as soon as possible. Sponge the area with undiluted white distilled vinegar and wash immediately afterward. For bad stains, add 250ml to 500ml (up to a pint) of vinegar to the wash cycle as well.

Water-soluble stains

Remove water-soluble stains (beer, fruit juices, black coffee, tea, vomit etc) from your cotton-blend clothing by patting the spot with a cloth moistened with undiluted white distilled vinegar just before placing it in the wash. For large stains, soak the garment overnight in a solution of 3 parts white distilled vinegar to 1 part cold water before washing.

Cleaning your Iron - *Inside*
To eliminate mineral deposits and prevent corrosion on your steam iron, give it an occasional cleaning by filling the reservoir with undiluted white distilled vinegar. Place the iron in an upright position, switch on the steam setting, and let the vinegar steam through it for 5-10 minutes. Then refill the chamber with clean water and repeat. Finally, give the water chamber a good rinsing with cold, clean water.

Cleaning your Iron - *Cleaning the soleplate*
To remove scorch marks from the soleplate of your iron, scrub it with a paste made by heating up equal parts white distilled vinegar and salt in a small pan. Use a rag dipped in clean water to wipe away the remaining residue.

Getting rid of old Hemlines
Moisten the area with a cloth dipped in equal parts white distilled vinegar and water, then place it under the garment before you start ironing.

Scorch marks
Eliminate slight scorch marks by rubbing the spot with a cloth dampened with white distilled vinegar, then blotting it with a clean towel.

Sharp creases
You'll find the creases in your freshly ironed clothes coming out a lot neater if you lightly spray them with equal parts water and white distilled vinegar before ironing them. For extra sharp creases in trouser and shirts, first dampen the garment using a cloth moistened in a solution of 1 part white distilled vinegar and 2 parts water. Then place a brown paper bag over the crease and start ironing.

Shiny seat marks
Brush the area lightly with a soft recycled toothbrush dipped in equal parts white distilled vinegar and water, then pat dry with a soft towel.

Wrinkle removal

Remove wrinkles out of clothes after drying by misting them with a solution of 1 part white distilled vinegar to 3 parts water. Spray the entire surface area thoroughly, hang it up and let it air-dry. You may find this approach works better for some clothes than ironing; it's certainly a lot gentler on the material.

Baby clothes

Baby Clothes

For babies with sensitive skin use half the recommended detergent during the wash and skip the fabric softener. Instead, put the clothes through an additional rinse at the end and fill the softener dispenser with white distilled vinegar. This both sterilizes and neutralizes any residue left by the detergent which may cause your baby's sensitive skin to react. If you also suffer from sensitive skin, follow the advice above for baby clothes and this could help prevent outbreaks and irritations.

Terry Nappies

Dilute 275 ml (1/2 pint) white distilled vinegar in 9 litres (approx 16 pints) of water and place in a nappy pail or bucket to neutralise the urine and help prevent staining. Soak and wash as usual.

Terry Nappies - *Prevent skin irritation*

Add 275ml (1/2 pint) white distilled vinegar during the rinse cycle to equalise the PH balance and help prevent skin irritation and nappy rash.

Vinegar is a great all purpose cleaner. Try these three recipes for creating your own cleaner for specific items.

For glass, stainless steel, and plastic laminate surfaces

Fill a recycled spray bottle with 2 parts water, 1 part distilled white vinegar, and a couple of drops of washing-up liquid. This will make an effective quick-clean solution.

For cleaning walls and other painted surfaces

Fill a recycled spray bottle with a cleaning solution made from 110ml (1/2 cup) white distilled vinegar, 225ml (1 cup) ammonia and 1/4 cup baking soda in 3.7 litres (1 gallon) water. Spritz it on spots and stains whenever needed and wipe off with a clean towel.

For cleaning pots and pans

To make an effective scouring mix which can be safely used on all of your metal cookware, including copper pots and pans, combine equal parts salt and flour and add just enough white distilled vinegar to make a paste. Work the paste around the cooking surface and the outside of the utensil, then rinse off with warm water and dry thoroughly with a soft dish towel.

Kitchen/Utility

Here are a collection of handy hints to keep your kitchen and utensils sparkling!

Aluminium cookware

To remove dark stains (caused by cooking acidic foods) mix 1 teaspoon of white distilled vinegar for every cup of water needed to cover the stains. Let it boil for a couple of minutes, then rinse with cold water.

Aluminium utensils

Bring back the shine by boiling in a solution of 2 tablespoons of white distilled vinegar in 1 3/4 pints (1 litre) of water.

Breadbox

Clean and disinfect by wiping with full strength white distilled vinegar. Also helps eliminate odours.

Bottles and decanters

Place a dessertspoon of salt in a bottle or decanter and moisten with white distilled vinegar. Shake vigorously and then rinse with cold water.

Ceramic Tiles - *Floor*

Add between 250 to 500ml (up to a pint) of white distilled vinegar to a bucket of water to mop ceramic floor tiles. This is quicker than mopping with detergent as no rinsing is needed.

Ceramic Tiles - *Wall*

Mix a solution of 1 part white distilled vinegar to 3 parts water and use a cloth to wipe tiles clean. This also preserves the colour of the grout.

China

Remove tea, coffee and other lingering stains from china by submerging in a cleaning solution made from boiling equal parts of white distilled vinegar and water. Soak for an hour and then rinse with clean water before use. For stubborn stains, try scrubbing with equal parts white distilled vinegar and salt. Rinse with warm clean water.

Cloths & Sponges

Keep cloths and sponges smelling fresh by soaking overnight in a solution of 55ml (1/4 cup) of white distilled vinegar and water. Rinse thoroughly before use.

Chrome

Apply a light misting of undiluted white vinegar from a recycled spray bottle. Buff with a soft cloth to bring out the brightness.

Coffeemaker

Fill the decanter with 450ml (2 cups) white distilled vinegar and 225ml (1 cup) water. Place a filter in the machine, and pour the solution into the coffeemaker's water chamber. Turn on the coffeemaker and let it run through a full brew cycle. Remove the filter and replace it with a fresh one. Then run clean water through the machine for two full cycles, replacing the filter again for the second brew.

Containers/Storage jars

Clean and disinfect by wiping with full strength white distilled vinegar.

Cutting Boards

Clean and disinfect by wiping with full strength white distilled vinegar.

Drains - *Deodorize*

Using a funnel, pour 115g (1/2 cup) of baking soda followed by 225ml (1 cup) of white distilled vinegar down the drain.

When the foaming subsides, flush with hot tap water. Wait five minutes, and then flush again with cold water. This will kill odour-causing bacteria.

Drains - *Improve drain speed*
To speed up a slow drain, pour in 115g (1/2 cup) of salt followed by 450ml (2 cups) of boiling white distilled vinegar. Flush through with hot and cold tap water.

Drains - *Unblock*
Following the methods above for deodorizing and improving drainage should also remove any blockage.

Egg Poacher
Prevent discolouration on egg poachers by adding 1 teaspoon of white distilled vinegar to the water when poaching eggs.

Fryer
Clean fat fryers after use by boiling out fat with an equal solution of water and white distilled vinegar. This is cost effective and safe, with no chemicals or risk of fire.

Frying Pan/Skillet
Boiling 450ml (2 cups) white distilled vinegar in your frying pan for 10 minutes will help keep food from sticking to it for several months at a time.

Glass - *Everyday use*
To rid drinking glasses of cloudiness or spots heat up a pot of equal parts of white distilled vinegar and water (use full-strength vinegar if your glasses are very cloudy), and let them soak in it for 15-30 minutes. Give them a good scrubbing with a bottle brush, then rinse clean.

Glass - *Crystal and Fine Cut Glass*
Add 225ml (1 cup) of white distilled vinegar to a basin of warm water. Gently dunk the glasses in the solution and allow to air-dry.

Dishwasher

General Cleaning

Remove built-up soap film and increase performance by pouring 225ml (1 cup) undiluted white distilled vinegar into the bottom of the unit, or in a bowl on the top rack. Then run the machine through a full cycle without any dishes or detergent. *Note: If there is no mention of vinegar in your dishwasher owner's manual, check with the manufacturer first.*

Dishwasher - *Glassware, Everyday*

Add 55ml (1/4 cup) white distilled vinegar in the rinse aid dispenser of the dishwasher to eliminate spots and cloudiness.

Dishwasher - *Glassware, Crystal and Fine Cut Glass*

Add 2 tablespoons of white distilled vinegar to dishwasher, then rinse in a solution of 3 parts warm water to 1 part white distilled vinegar and allow to air-dry.

Glass ovenware

Fill ovenware with 1 part white distilled vinegar and 4 parts water and heat the mixture to a slow boil. Let it boil at a low level for five minutes. The stains should come off with some mild scrubbing once the mixture cools.

Grease Splatters

Remove grease splatters from all of your kitchen surfaces by washing them with a sponge dipped in undiluted white distilled vinegar. Use another sponge soaked in cold tap water to rinse, then wipe dry with a soft cloth.

Grease and food stains in saucepans (burnt-on)

Soften with a solution of 225ml (1 cup) apple cider vinegar and 2 tablespoons of sugar. Apply the mixture while the pan is still hot, and let it sit for an hour or so.

Grill Hoods/Extractor Fans

Use undiluted white distilled vinegar to cut through the grease on grill hoods and extractor fan covers.

Hob/Hotplate

Wipe with full strength white distilled vinegar to remove food stains.

Ice trays

To remove water spots or disinfect your trays, let them soak in undiluted white distilled vinegar for four to five hours, then rinse well under cold water and let dry.

Kettle

To remove limescale from your kettle, fill kettle with water and add 100ml (approx 1/2 cup) of white distilled vinegar. Let it stand overnight, then rinse well with clean water.

Microwave - *General cleaning*

To clean your microwave, place a glass bowl filled with a solution of 55ml (1/4 cup) vinegar in 225ml (1 cup) water inside the microwave and zap the mixture for five minutes on the highest setting. Once the bowl cools, dip a cloth or sponge into the liquid and use it to wipe away stains and splatters on the interior.

Microwave - *Odour removal*

Place 1 tablespoon of white wine vinegar in a microwave proof cup and heat in microwave to boiling, to elimate lingering odours.

Non-stick cookware

For mineral stains on your nonstick cookware, rub the utensil with a cloth dipped in undiluted white distilled vinegar. To loosen up stubborn stains, mix 2 tablespoons baking soda, 100ml (approx 1/2 cup) of white distilled vinegar, and 225ml (1 cup) of water and let it boil for 10 minutes.

Odours - *Cooking Smells*

Remove lingering cooking smells by filling a small bowl or cup full of undiluted distilled white vinegar, which will absorb unwanted odours.

Refrigerator

Clean and disinfect by wiping with full strength white distilled vinegar to remove any potentially harmful bacteria.

Saucepans, skillets.

To remove stubborn stains, fill pan with equal parts of white distilled vinegar and water and bring to boil. Rinse thoroughly with clean water before use.

Scissors

When your scissor blades get sticky or grimy, don't use water to wash them off; you're far more likely to rust the fastener that holds the blades together - or the blades themselves - than get them clean. Instead, wipe down the blades with a cloth dipped in full-strength white distilled vinegar, and then dry with a rag or dish towel.

Stainless steel cookware

Soak in 450ml (2 cups) of white distilled vinegar for 30 minutes, then rinse with hot, soapy water followed by a cold-water rinse.

Stainless steel

To clean stainless steel fixtures around your home, apply a light misting of undiluted white vinegar from a recycled spray bottle. Buff with a soft cloth to bring out the brightness.

Tea Pot

Clean tea pots by boiling equal parts of white distilled vinegar and water for several minutes and let stand an hour. Then rinse with clean water.

Thermos flask

Fill with warm water and 50ml (approx. 1/4 cup) white distilled vinegar then add some uncooked rice, which will act as an abrasive. Close and shake well, then rinse and let it air-dry.

Vinyl Flooring

Add 100ml (approx 1/2 cup) of white distilled vinegar to a bucket of water to keep your vinyl floors clean. Not only does it keep the floors shiny but it kills the dust mites.

Washing-up liquid

Pour 3-4 tablespoons white distilled vinegar into your favourite brand (especially bargain brands) of washing-up liquid and give it a few shakes. The added vinegar will not only increase the detergent's grease-fighting capabilities, but also provide you with more dishwashing liquid for the money.

Waxing Floors

When waxing a floor after scrubbing with a floor stripper, add 225ml (1 cup) of white distilled vinegar to rinse water. It neutralizes the chemicals and makes wax or floor finish adhere better.

Work Surface

Clean and disinfect by wiping with full strength white distilled vinegar.

Oven - *General Cleaning*

To remove grease and grime and cooking spills from inside your oven, make a paste of 225ml (1 cup) white distilled vinegar and 30g (1/4 cup) of powdered laundry detergent.

Heat your oven for five minutes at 180 degrees and turn off. Spread the paste around the oven, applying it more heavily to very greasy areas. Leave paste on for an hour, then use a plastic spatula to gently scrape the dirt away.

Odours - *Neutralize chemical odours*

If you choose to clean your oven with chemical cleaners, keep your freshly-cleaned oven from stinking up your house next time you cook something, by wiping it with white distilled vinegar poured directly on the sponge as a final rinse. It neutralizes the harsh alkali of oven cleaners.

Oven - *Odour removal*

Stop unpleasant cooking odours from permeating through the house whilst cooking. Boil 225ml (1 cup) of white distilled vinegar with 450ml (2 cups) of water in a pan on the hob. Leave boiling until the liquid is almost gone.

Oven - *Prevent build up of grease in Oven*

Dip a sponge or cloth in full strength white distilled vinegar and wipe down all sides of the oven to prevent a greasy build up.

Bath

Clean thoroughly with a cloth or sponge dipped in full-strength white distilled vinegar, to ensure bacteria removal and extra shine. Rinse thoroughly with cold water.

Bath - *Water marks*

To remove hard-water stains pour in 675ml (3 cups) of distilled white vinegar under a running hot tap water. Allow the bathtub to fill up over the stains and allow it to soak for about four hours. When the water drains out, you should be able to easily scrub off the stains.

Bathroom Cabinet/Mirror

Clean and disinfect by wiping with a cloth dipped in white distilled vinegar.

Ceramic Tiles

Mix a solution of 1 part white distilled vinegar to 3 parts water and use a cloth to wipe tiles clean. This also preserves the colour of the grout.

Chrome fixtures

Apply a light misting of undiluted white vinegar from a recycled spray bottle. Buff with a soft cloth to bring out the brightness.

Grout

Dip an old toothbrush in undiluted white vinegar and scrub grout to remove grubbiness and restore to its original colour.

Hard water spots

To remove hard water spots from sinks, showers and baths, wipe using a cloth soaked in full-strength vinegar. Allow to stand for about five minutes and then rinse with clean water.

Limescale deposit

Heat a small container of white distilled vinegar to boiling point. Then pour over your fixtures that have deposits of limescale. This will release or remove the deposit.

Mould and mildew

Mix a solution of 3 tablespoons of white distilled vinegar, 1 teaspoon borax, and 450ml (2 cups) of hot water into a clean, recycled spray bottle and give it a few good shakes. Spray the solution onto the affected area and allow to soak in. For stubborn stains, use a soft scrubbing brush. Wipe away with a clean cloth.

The solution is suitable for mould and mildew removal on painted surfaces, tiles, windows, or wherever you see mould or mildew spots.

Rinse cup

Fill with equal parts water and white distilled vinegar, or just full-strength vinegar, and let it sit overnight. Rinse thoroughly with cold water before using.

Shower curtain

Remove mildew from your shower curtain by placing it in your washing machine with a couple of towels. Add 110ml (1/2 cup) of liquid laundry detergent and 115g (1/2 cup) of baking soda to the load, and wash it in warm water on your machine's regular cycle.

Add 225ml (1 cup) white distilled vinegar to the first rinse. Before the machine goes into the spin cycle, remove the curtain and let it hang-dry.

Shower doors - glass

Wipe with a cloth dipped in a solution of 110ml (1/2 cup) of white distilled vinegar, 225ml (1 cup) of ammonia, and 60g (1/4 cup) of baking soda mixed in about 4 litres of warm water.

Shower door - tracks

Fill the tracks with approximately 450ml (2 cups) of full-strength white vinegar and let it sit for three to five hours. If the tracks are really dirty, heat the vinegar in a glass container for 30 seconds in your microwave first. Then pour some hot water over the track to flush away the gunk.

Shower heads - *removable*

Remove blockages and mineral deposits from showerheads by placing them in 1 litre of hot water with 110ml (1/2 cup) white distilled vinegar for 10 minutes.

Shower heads - *fixed*

Fill a small plastic bag half full with white distilled vinegar and tape it over the fixture. Let it sit for about 1 hour, then remove the bag and wipe off any excess.

Sink - *Porcelain*

Clean thoroughly with a cloth dipped in full-strength white distilled vinegar, to ensure bacteria removal and extra shine. Rinse thoroughly with cold water.

Sink - *Porcelain, water marks*

To remove hard-water stains pour in 225ml (1 cup) of white distilled vinegar under running hot tap water. Allow the sink to fill up over the stains and allow it to soak for about four hours.

Soap build-up

To remove soap scum and build up from sinks, showers and baths, wipe with a cloth soaked in full-strength vinegar. Allow to stand for about five minutes and then rinse with clean water. Get the grime and soap build up out of the grooves of your soap dish by cleaning with a cloth dipped in white distilled vinegar.

Taps

Remove grime and dirt that builds up around the base of taps by soaking paper towels in full-strength white distilled vinegar and then wrap the towels around the fixtures. Leave for about an hour and then remove towels and clean as usual.

Toilet bowl

Pour 450ml (2 cups) of white distilled vinegar into the bowl and let the solution soak overnight before flushing. This will also remove water rings that typically appear just above the water level.

Toothbrush holder

Get the grime and caked-on toothpaste drippings out of the grooves by cleaning with a cloth moistened with white distilled vinegar.

Air freshener

Mix 1 teaspoon of baking soda, 1 tablespoon of distilled white vinegar and 450ml (2 cups of water). After it stops foaming, mix well, and spritz into the air using a spray bottle.

Ballpoint-pen marks

Dab some full-strength distilled white vinegar on the ballpoint pen mark using a cloth or a sponge. Repeat until the marks are gone.

Blinds - *Venetian or slatted*

Put on a white cotton glove and moisten the fingers in a solution made of equal parts white vinegar and hot tap water. Now simply slide your fingers across both sides of each slat and prepare to be amazed. Use a container of clean water to periodically wash off the glove.

Brass, Bronze and Copper

Clean brass, bronze, copper objects and doorware by making a paste of equal parts distilled white vinegar and salt, or vinegar and baking soda (wait for the fizzing to stop before using). Use a clean, soft cloth or paper towel to rub the paste into the item until the tarnish is gone. Then rinse with cool water and polish with a soft towel until dry.

Brickwork

Wipe with a damp mop dipped in 225ml (1 cup) of white vinegar mixed with approximately 4 litres of warm water. You can also use this same solution to brighten up the bricks around your fireplace.

Candle wax

To remove candle wax first soften the wax using a blow-dryer on its hottest setting and blot up as much as you can with paper towels. Then remove what's left by rubbing with a cloth soaked in a solution made of equal parts distilled white vinegar and water. Wipe clean with a soft, absorbent cloth.

Carpets and Rugs

Prevent mildew from forming on the bottoms of rugs and carpeting by misting the backs with full-strength white vinegar from a spray bottle. If your rugs or carpets are looking worn and dingy from too much foot traffic bring them back to life by brushing them with a clean broom dipped in a solution of 225ml (1 cup) of distilled white vinegar in 4 litres of water. Your faded threads will perk up, and you don't even need to rinse off the solution. To remove stains, fill a trigger spray bottle with one part distilled white vinegar to five parts water. Take a second spray bottle and fill with one part white, non sudsy amonnia and five parts water. Saturate stain with vinegar solution. Allow to soak in for a few minutes and blot thoroughly with a clean cloth. Then go over the area with the ammonia solution, leave to soak in and then and blot again. Repeat until the stain is gone.

Chewing gum

Remove chewing gum from textiles by saturating the area in distilled white vinegar. Heat the vinegar first, either in the microwave or on the hob, and this will make it will work faster.

Cupboard - *musty odour*

Remove the contents then wash with a cloth dampened in a solution of 225ml (1 cup) each of white distilled vinegar and ammonia and 60g (1/4 cup) of baking soda in 4 litres of water. Leave doors open to dry completely.

Fireplaces

Create an equal part mix of water and white distilled vinegar to remove the blackened soot on glass front doors. If the doors have a spring-loaded clip, remove it, then take out the doors. Lay them flat on newspapers, spray with the vinegar/water solution and soak. Wipe it off with newspaper.

Glue - *Acetate, Fiberglass, Rayon, Silk, Triacetate, Wool*

Immediately sponge the area with water. Then apply a wet spotter and a few drops of white vinegar. To prepare a wet spotter, mix 1 part glycerine, 1 part white dishwashing detergent, and 8 parts water. Shake well before each use. Store wet spotter in a plastic squeeze bottle. Cover with an absorbent pad dampened with wet spotter. Let it stand as long as any stain is being picked up. Change the pad as it removes the stain. Keep both the stain and pad moist with wet spotter and vinegar. Repeat until no more stain is removed.

Leather sofas and chairs

Make a cleaning solution from equal parts of white distilled vinegar and boiled linseed oil in a recycled spray bottle. Shake the bottle well and spray lightly and evenly over your furniture. Rub it off with a clean cloth. To remove watermarks and water rings moisten a sponge with white distilled vinegar and dab gently, ensuring that you completely cover the area affected by the mark.

Mirrors

To make a homemade anti-fogging glass cleaner suitable for mirrors and glassware, place 1 part white distilled vinegar to 3 parts water in a spray bottle and mist. Wipe with a soft lint free cloth.

Silver

Make your silverware - as well as your pure silver bracelets, rings, and other jewellery - shine like new by soaking them in a mixture of 110ml (1/2 cup) of white distilled vinegar and 2 tablespoons of baking soda for two to three hours. Rinse them under cold water and dry thoroughly with a soft cloth.

Smoke odour

Remove lingering smoky odour by placing a shallow bowl about three quarters full of white or cider vinegar in the room where the scent is strongest. Use several bowls if the smell permeates your entire home. The odour should be gone in less than a day.

Stickers

To remove a sticker affixed to painted furniture or a painted wall, simply saturate the corners and sides of the sticker with full strength white vinegar and carefully scrape it off (using an expired credit card or a plastic phone card). Remove any sticky remains by pouring on a bit more vinegar. Let it sit for a minute or two, and then wipe with a clean cloth. This approach is equally effective for removing price tags and other stickers from glass, plastic, and other glossy surfaces.

Walls and Woodwork

You can ease the job of washing painted walls and woodwork by using a mixture of 225ml (1 cup) ammonia, 110ml (1/2 cup) white distilled or cider vinegar and 60g (1/4 cup) of baking soda with about 4 litres of warm water. Wipe this solution over walls or blinds with a sponge or cloth and rinse with clean water.

Windows

Simply wash with a mixture of equal parts of white distilled vinegar and warm water. Dry with a soft cloth. This solution will make your windows gleam and will not leave the usual film or streaks on the glass.

Wood furniture

Conceal scratches by mixing some white distilled vinegar and iodine in a small jar and paint over the scratch with a small artist's brush. Use more iodine for darker woods; more vinegar for lighter shades. To remove white rings left by wet glasses on wood furniture, mix equal parts white distilled vinegar and olive oil and apply it with a soft cloth while moving with the wood grain. Use another clean, soft cloth to shine it up. To remove the build up of wax and polish dip a cloth in equal parts white distilled vinegar and water and squeeze it out well. Then, moving with the grain, clean away the polish.

Wood panelling - *revitalize*

Mix 1 pint of warm water, 4 tablespoons of white or apple cider vinegar, and 2 tablespoons olive oil in a container, give it a couple of shakes, and apply with a clean cloth. Let the mixture soak into the wood for several minutes, then polish with a dry cloth

Concrete - *handcare*

Even though you wear rubber gloves when working with concrete, some of the stuff inevitably splashes on your skin. Prolonged contact with wet concrete can cause your skin to crack. Use undiluted white distilled vinegar to wash dried concrete or mortar off your skin, then wash with warm, soapy water.

Fixings - *Loosening*

Pour white distilled vinegar on rusted hinges and screws to loosen them up for removal.

Painting

To achieve the best results for your paintwork, it is essential to remove all dust and grime so simply wipe over with a cloth moistened with a solution made from 1 part white distilled vinegar to 3 parts water. Allow to dry before beginning to paint. If you have an accident and paint ends up on your windows, just heat up the white distilled vinegar either in a microwave or on the hob and use a cloth to wipe away paint. Painted cement floors have a tendency to peel after a while. But you can keep the paint stuck to the cement longer by giving the floor an initial coat of white distilled vinegar before you paint it. Wait until the vinegar has dried, then begin painting. You can also reduce peeling on painted metal surfaces by wiping down with a vinegar solution made of 1 part white distilled vinegar to 5 parts water prior to painting.

Paint Brushes - *Softening*

Bring a pan of white distilled vinegar to the boil on the hob and allow brushes to simmer for around 5 minutes. Remove from the pan and wash in hot soapy water.

Paint fumes

Place a couple of shallow dishes filled with undiluted white distilled vinegar around a freshly painted room to quickly get rid of the strong paint smell.

Plaster

If you add a couple of teaspoons of white distilled vinegar to your plaster mix, this will allow you more time to work the plaster before it hardens.

Radiators

Turn down the thermostat. Unscrew the air vent, soak it in white distilled vinegar to clean it, then turn the thermostat all the way up. After a few minutes, you'll hear a hissing sound followed by a little bit of water spurting out. Finally, steam will start exiting that hole. Turn off the radiator valve and replace the vent. It should be straight up and hand tight.

Remove glue from furniture joints

To loosen old glue from around the rungs and joints of tables and chairs you are repairing or renovating, apply full-strength white distilled vinegar directly onto the joint.

Rust

To remove rust from bolts and other metals, soak them in full strength white distilled vinegar. If you want to clean up those rusted old tools you recently unearthed in your garage or picked up at a boot sale, soak them in full-strength white distilled vinegar for several days to remove rust, dirt and grime.

Varnished Wood

A "cloudy" appearance on varnished wood can be removed easily, assuming the cloudiness hasn't gone through to the wood, by rubbing the surface with a cloth moistened with a solution of 1 tablespoon of white distilled vinegar and 1 litre of warm water. Ensure that there is no excess moisture on the cloth by wringing out thoroughly before use, and then complete the job by drying the surface with a soft cloth or rag.

Wallpaper

Spray white distilled vinegar directly onto the surface of the wallpaper and leave for a few minutes, then try removing the paper with a scraper. If it won't shift that easily try scoring the paper then spray again.

Woodstain

White distilled vinegar can be mixed with water-based inks to make a simple stain for wood. Pour vinegar into a mixing jar, add the ink until the desired colour is achieved and apply to wood with a brush or rag.

Animal deterrent

Some animals (including cats, deer, dogs, rabbits, and foxes) dislike the scent of vinegar even after it has dried. You can keep these unauthorized visitors out of your garden by soaking several recycled rags in full-strength white distilled vinegar, and placing them on stakes around your garden, particularly around areas such as vegetable patches and flower beds. Resoak the rags approximately every 7-10 days.

Antibacterial hand spray

If you prefer not to wear gloves while gardening – carry a spray bottle with white distilled vinegar with you and if you scratch yourself, spray it with the solution straight away which should prevent infection.

Birds

Remove bird droppings by spraying them with full-strength apple cider vinegar. Or pour the vinegar onto a rag and wipe them off. Use vinegar to deter birds building their mud nests in your facias. When you see that they are interested in building where they are not wanted, drench the area with full-strength white distilled vinegar. They will probably try several more times to make a nest. Keep spraying the area with vinegar as they become discouraged after several attempts and go elsewhere. Under no circumstances spray the birds.

Brickwork

To get rid of calcium buildup on brick or on limestone, use a spray bottle with half white distilled vineger and half water, then just let it set. The solution will do all the work.

Climbing frames and swings

Clean and disinfect regularly by washing with a solution of 1 part white distilled vinegar and 1 part water.

Decking

Mix a solution of 225ml (1 cup) of ammonia, 110ml (1/2 cup) of white vinegar, and 60g (1/2 cup) of baking soda mixed in 4 litres of water. Use a bristle brush or broom dipped in the solution and brush onto the deck to remove mildew.

Drains

To "green clean" your drains without the use of harsh chemicals, pour 60g (1/2 cup) of baking soda and 110ml (1/2 cup) of white distilled vinegar down the drain and then cover whilst the solution fizzes. Follow this with a bucket of very hot or boiling water.

Garden Furniture - *cane and wicker*

Sponge furniture with a solution of 1 part white distilled vinegar and 1 part hot water. Place the chairs out in the hot sun to dry and this will clean and improve the appearance of sagging.

Garden Furniture - *mesh and umbrellas*

To deodorize and inhibit mildew growth on outdoor plastic mesh furniture and patio umbrellas, mix 450m (2 cups) of white vinegar and 2 tablespoons of liquid detergent in a bucket of hot water. Use a soft brush to work it into the grooves of the plastic as well as for scrubbing seat pads and umbrella fabric. Rinse with cold water; then dry in the sun.

Garden Furniture - *plastic*

Spray with full-strength white vinegar and wipe with a cloth. This will remove dirt build up and mildew and the vinegar should prevent the mildew reappearing for a while.

Garden Furniture - *wood*

Mix a solution of 225ml (1 cup) of ammonia, 110ml (1/2 cup) of white vinegar, and 60g (1/2 cup) of baking soda mixed in 4 litres of water. Soak a sponge or rag in the solution and wipe down the furniture to remove mildew.

Greenhouse glass

Mix 3 tablespoons of white distilled vinegar with 1/2 teaspoon of liquid detergent and 575ml (1 pint) of water and decant into a trigger spray bottle. Lightly mist the glass and then wipe dry with a paper towel and polish with newspaper for a fantastic shine. This solution works on all glass surfaces.

Insects - *fixed trap*

If the bugs are feasting on the fruits and vegetables in your garden, fill a 2 litre plastic bottle with 225ml (1 cup) of apple cider vinegar and 120g (1 cup) of sugar. Next, slice up a banana peel into small pieces and put these into the bottle with 225ml (1 cup) of cold water and shake it up. Tie a piece of string around the neck of the bottle and hang it from a low tree branch, or place it on the ground, to trap and kill insects. Replace used traps with new ones as needed.

Insects - *portable trap*

If you are hosting a barbecue or party in the garden and want to ensure that your guests are not plagued by flying insects (gnats, flies, mosquitoes etc) place a bowl filled with apple cider vinegar near some food, but away from you and your guests. By the evening's end, most of your uninvited guests will be floating inside the bowl.

Insect repellant

If you have problems with ants and other insects invading your home, they are probably crossing your door and/or window sills and baseboards. Pour full-strength white distilled vinegar around these areas and this will prevent the insects invading - for some reason, they will not cross it!

Lawns - *brown patches*

If your lawn suffers from brown patches caused by dog urine, place a few drops of white distilled vinegar in your dog's water bowl every day and this will neutralize the acidity in the urine and lessen the likelihood of brown patches appearing. Alternatively if you catch your dog "in the act", mix a solution of equal parts white distilled vinegar and water and spray this liberally over the area where your dog has been which should help.

Lawn mower blades

Grass, especially when it's damp, has a tendency to accumulate on your lawn mower blades after you cut the lawn. Wipe down the blades with a cloth dampened with undiluted white distilled vinegar. It will clean off leftover grass on the blades, as well as any insects.

Patios, Paths and Driveways

Spray unwanted weeds with full-strength white distilled vinegar or apple cider vinegar. Give each plant a single spritz of vinegar in its midsection, or in the middle of the flower before the plants go to seed. Aim another shot near the stem at ground level so the vinegar can soak down to the roots. Keep an eye on the weather, though; if it rains the next day, you'll need to give the weeds another spraying.

Pesticide

If you have a slug problem, drop a few drops (an eye dropper works well) of white distilled vinegar on them and they will dissolve. But be careful not to get the vinegar on plants, it will kill them. Mealybugs are the most insidious and common pests on both houseplants and in the garden. Stop the invasion by dabbing the insects with a cotton swab dipped in full-strength white distilled vinegar which will kill the insects and any eggs left behind.

Plant diseases - *rust, black spot, and powdery mildew*
Mix 2 tablespoons of apple cider vinegar in 2 litres of water, and pour some into a recycled spray bottle. Spray the solution on your affected plants in the morning or early evening (when temperatures are relatively cool and there's no direct light on the plant) until the condition is cured.

Plant diseases - *yellow leaves on plants*
The sudden appearance of yellow leaves on plants accustomed to acidic soils - such as azaleas, hydrangeas, and gardenias - could signal a drop in the plant's iron intake or a shift in the ground's pH.

Either problem can be resolved by watering the soil around the afflicted plants once a week for three weeks with 225ml (1 cup) of a solution made by mixing 2 tablespoons of apple cider vinegar in 1 litre of water.

Soil

If you have alkaline soil and are trying to grow rhododendrons, gardenias, azaleas or other acid loving plants, add 1 1/2 tablespoons of white distilled vinegar to 2 litres of water, and water thoroughly.

Soil - *acidity test*
To do a quick test for excess acidity in your soil place a handful of earth in a container and then pour in 110ml (1/2 cup) of white distilled vinegar and 60g (1/2 cup) of baking soda. If the soil fizzes or bubbles, it is definitely acidic.

Soil - *alkalinity test*
To do a quick test for excess alkalinity in your soil place a handful of earth in a container and then pour in 110ml (1/2 cup) of white distilled vinegar. If the soil fizzes or bubbles, it is definitely alkaline.

Brush

Clean your pet's brush and comb by dipping in apple cider vinegar and then rinsing with cold water. This will stop bacteria forming.

Cat Litter tray odour

When you have washed the litter tray, rinse it out and pour about 1/2 inch of full-strength white distilled vinegar into the tray. Let it stand for 20 minutes or so, then swish it around, rinse with cold water, and dry the box. The acid in the vinegar neutralizes the ammonia smell. If kitty has had an accident on washable material, mix 110-225ml/1/2-1 cup of white distilled vinegar to your laundry, and wash as normal.

Coat conditioner - *cat or dog*

Add a teaspoon of apple cider vinegar to your cat or dog's drinking water which will provide additional nutrients to its diet, giving it a shinier and healthier-looking coat.

Dog Blanket

For damp doggy smells, when you next wash the dog blanket add 110ml/1/2 cup white distilled water to the final rinse cycle of your washing machine to remove odours.

Dog Toys

Clean and disinfect your dog toys regularly with this natural antibiotic. Soak the toys in apple cider vinegar for 10-15 minutes and then rinse in cold water. Allow to dry naturally.

Ear Cleaning

Mix 1/3 rubbing alcohol and 1/3 white distilled vinegar and 1/3 water to create an ear cleaning solution for your cat or dog. Using a dropper, squirt 8-10 drops in ear holding head to side; let it stand in the ear for a minute then drain. While holding their head tilted, massage the ear around in a circle then tilt and wipe out with tissue. Apply once a month or if your animal is scratching. However, if after cleaning the scratching persists they have mites or a bacterial infection and you should take them to the vet.

Fleas

Add a teaspoon of apple cider vinegar to your dog or cat's drinking water which will act as a natural deterrent to fleas and ticks. Directly protect your dog against fleas and ticks - fill a spray bottle with equal parts water and apple cider vinegar and apply it directly to the dog's coat and rub it in well. This is safe to use on puppies too.

Hip dysplasia

Apple cider vinegar breaks down calcium deposits while re-mineralizing bones, and can be used for dogs who suffer from hip dysplasia. Put a teaspoon in with their drinking water daily.

Housetraining

When housetraining a puppy or kitten, it will often wet previously soiled spots. After cleaning up the mess, it is essential to remove the scent from your floor, carpeting, or sofa, and nothing does the job better than vinegar. Blot up as much of the stain as possible. Then mop with equal parts white distilled vinegar and warm water. On a wood or vinyl floor, test a few drops of vinegar in an inconspicuous area to make sure it won't harm the finish. Dry with a cloth or paper towel.

The hints, tips and recipes contained in this book are passed on in good faith but the publisher cannot be held responsible for any adverse results. Spoon measurements are level, teaspoons are assumed to be 5ml, tablespoons 15ml. For other measurements, see chart below.

Spoons to millilitres

1/2 teaspoon	2.5 ml	1 Tablespoon	15 ml
1 teaspoon	5 ml	2 Tablespoons	30 ml
1-1 1/2 teaspoons	7.5 ml	3 Tablespoons	45 ml
2 teaspoons	10 ml	4 Tablespoons	60 ml

Grams to ounces

10g	0.25oz	225g	8oz
15g	0.38oz	250g	9oz
25g	1oz	275g	10oz
50g	2oz	300g	11oz
75g	3oz	350g	12oz
110g	4oz	375g	13oz
150g	5oz	400g	14oz
175g	6oz	425g	15oz
200g	7oz	350g	16oz

Metric to cups

Description		1 cup
Flour etc	115g	1 cup
Clear honey etc	350g	1 cup
Liquids etc	225ml	1 cup

Liquid measures

5fl oz	1/4 pint	150 ml
7.5fl oz		215 ml
10fl oz	1/2 pint	275 ml
15fl oz		425 ml
20fl oz	1 pint	570 ml
35fl oz		1 litre

This edition first published in 2009 by ImPulse Paperbacks, an imprint of Iron Press Ltd. © Iron Press Ltd 2009 Printed in China